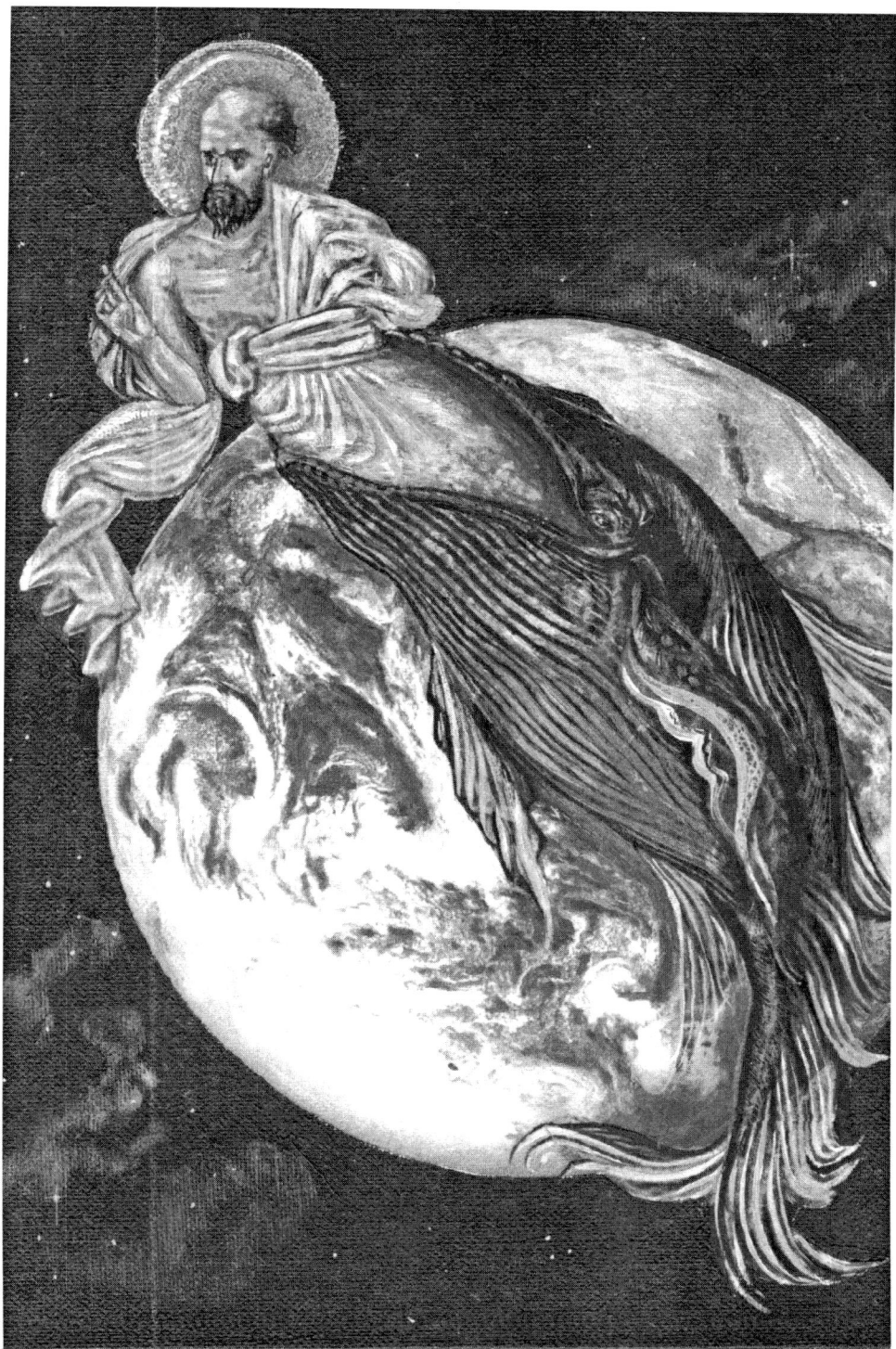

Jonah

A Prophecy at the Millennium

Jonah
A Prophecy at the Millennium

by

Albert J. LaChance

with an Introduction by
Carol Wallas LaChance

DORRANCE PUBLISHING CO., INC.
PITTSBURGH, PENNSYLVANIA 15222

ISBN # 0-8059-4007-3
Printed in the United States of America

First Printing

For information or to order additional books, please write:
Dorrance Publishing Co., Inc.
643 Smithfield Street
Pittsburgh, Pennsylvania 15222
U.S.A.

Dedication

To my wife, Carol, who knows all my secret meanings.

Table of Contents

	Introduction ---------------------------------------ix
Poems # 1-5	The Call --- 1
Poems # 6-9	The Joy of Life ------------------------------------ 7
Poems # 10-17	The Way of Sorrow and Death ---------------- 11
Poem # 18	Meeting the Father ----------------------------- 21
Poems # 19-23	Resurrection and the Goddess ----------------- 23
Poems # 24-29	The New Story ---------------------------------- 29
Poem # 30	A Warning from the Earth ---------------------- 39
	Epilogue --- 43

The word of the Lord came to Jonah:
"Set out for the great city of
Nineveh, and announce to it the
message that I will tell you." So
Jonah made ready and went to
Nineveh according to the Lord's bidding.
Jonah 3:1-3

"This is an evil age. It seeks a
sign. But no sign will be given it
except the sign of Jonah."
Luke 11:29

Introduction

Spirit dreams and a human child is born.
Soul and body are one epiphany. Before time,
Before light, before life from light became,
This thought was, this flesh was, and this
Thought, this flesh became life of you and me.
We two, in love, are one epiphany. O my child,
Mind and matter, soul and body, woman and man,
These are one epiphany.

On a cold January morning, just before dawn, I gave birth to our second daughter, Kateri, in our bedroom. My husband, Albert, gently guided our child into the world, cradling her in his hands for a moment, before passing her to me. Through the long night he had been with me, encouraging me, ministering to my pain, laughing and sharing as we awaited this little one. He was the midwife who stood guard at those powerful moments. Birthing our daughters together remain the supreme moments of my life. In the same way, the poem that you are about to read, written by Albert over the first eleven years of our marriage, is a shared birthing, one at which I was privileged to be the midwife.

I first met Albert LaChance in a class he was teaching on creative writing. He was, and still is, a dynamic and fascinating lecturer. For several weeks I sat in the back of the room mesmerized. For the first time in years my spirit awoke. I remember we listened to T.S. Eliot reading "The Four Quartets," and Albert's reverence for Eliot's vision was tangible. As the class continued, Albert discovered through one of my writing assignments that I was from England. He begged me to read his poetry aloud to the class so he could hear them read with an English accent! Thus fittingly, our relationship began; a love affair inspired by, and built upon, a foundation of poetry. *Jonah* was conceived and brought to birth through the synthesis of Albert's three great loves: God, Thomas Stearns Eliot, and me. I do not know what I did to deserve such good company! But I do know that later we journeyed together to God and to T.S. Eliot's grave at Westminster Abbey.

It is difficult to adequately describe the level of discipline and commitment that a creative work of this magnitude demands. Poetry at this level comes from the depths of a person and requires a complete surrender to the process. It cannot be made to order. It requires a way of life that is focused totally on being obedient to the poetry. *Jonah* took nine years to write—each poem had its own long and difficult gestation period. Like a woman carrying a child, Albert never knew when the "contractions" for a particular poem would begin. Nor did I! Like physical contractions, the opening of the heart and soul to allow the poems to be birthed was often accompanied by deep pain and despair. Once the words finally emerged on the pages, we would celebrate, forgetting the struggle of the process.

Jonah is the journey of one man's inner initiation, a spiritual journey from joy through despair and into resurrection and new birth. Our married life provides many of the images for the poem, thus Albert's dedication to me as the one who "knows all my secret meanings." For you, the reader, this poem will hint at multiple meanings and images, which will be unique to you. However, there are three keys that will help you to fully unlock the meaning and structure of the poem. Firstly, the journey motif follows the pattern of Joseph Campbell's "hero journey." A reading of "The Hero With a Thousand Faces" will help explore the architecture of the poems. Secondly, the resurrection sequence which contains the new cosmology is inspired by the work of Albert's great teacher, Father Thomas Berry. His book *The Dream of the Earth* contains an essay called "The New Story" which is highly recommended. These two mentors, together with T.S. Eliot, have deeply informed Albert's mystical vision. But, I know that if you were to ask Albert, he would say that the real power behind the poetry is always the author of all life, Jesus Christ.

As I write, the cherry tree I gave Albert when the last poem was written stands tall in our garden, offering shade and blossoms. Our married life is still a journey, groping always toward a fuller expression of love for God and each other. The everyday demands of life absorb us. Still, every so often it is possible to stop, and by reading these poems enter again into a deeper reality, and remember that "the mind dreaming everywhere is dreaming here." Our journey through life is never taken alone.

Take time with these words. Read them aloud, slowly. Let their images awaken you. This is not a book to read once, but rather a journey to take often. It is best taken slowly, consciously adjusting to the earth's time and rhythms as it is read. The promise of the piece is that it will unfold its mysteries to you the more you read it. Deep within you, the reader, the memories of the Earth and Cosmos, the great Dream of God, will be revealed once again.

> Memories, as soft as the stroke
> of a robin's breast, memories...
> the lilac, dahlia, the magnolia
> the rose, the pear tree sighing
> her petals in the moonlit dawn.

Carol Wallas LaChance
November 1996
Goffstown, New Hampshire

The Call

In August, the summer in full flourish,
The Casino would be laughing from the gut:
Pinball pizza popcorn balloons. The mob
Would be smiling, gold-toothed, tanned, arrayed
In splashes of yellow, orange, and red
Gaudy, a la Hawaii…walking their
Strutting yappers: poodles, Pomeranians,
And Pekingese; forms and forms flowing over
The pavement, dreams drifting through the heat…
But this is February.
                    The two clocks, frozen,
Stare seaward to the North Atlantic. Out
Of time, wrongly they measure time staring…
Seaward toward the sand…toward the empty spirit
The clear space of sky…toward the lunging
Of relentless waves…toward the death-cold ocean
And the moon…toward the pale translucence of
The February moon in the pastel terror
Of this winter afternoon…toward…
The jetty.
          This is New Hampshire.
                              The Casino
Is locked and barred with latches and padlocks.
The noise, the commotion and people are gone
To where noise people and commotion go.
The laughter, the colors, the smiles, the dogs
Gone…with all the comforts of the summer heat.
Gone…leaving only the wind crying down the empty
Street, the wind…chasing—CLUP—CLUP—CLUP—
An empty paper cup that echoes our footsteps
As we walk…
            toward the jetty.
                        This is February…

The wind has made the beach a whirling
Horizon of snakes, preceding and warning
Of the jetty. The sand is littered
With refuse of the warmer times:
Cigar butts, beer bottles, burst balloons.
A book opens and closes with the wind.
The sand is breathing bubbles…
There are living beings below.
Unopened wine, uneaten bread remind
Of our forgotten food…a child's doll
Stares skyward, forgotten or abandoned
At the lips of the sea.
                              We approach the jetty
And the sea begins to speak, not the cry
Of the gull nor the horn, the way mountains
And valleys speak, mountains and valleys
Of a hidden terrain that is realms and realms
Beneath the waves that knock the rocking boat
Against the sky…down and down…fathoms
And fathoms down, where the whale moans among
Shadows, among histories and pre-histories of ruins.
And this voice whispering from the deep draws
All with ears to hear it toward the jetty.

Stone is heaped on stone, boulder on boulder.
The mind extends its timid reach down the jetty
Toward the heaving deeps. The sea strikes
Beat upon beat hurling wind-driven waves
That crest smash and splash back
The salty wash coughing out rocks, weeds and mud
That shatter the ice clinging between the stones.
                    This is February…
The wind shrieks…gulls are stilled
                    —midflight—   fly
Backward. Screaming sand abrades the face
Mucous and tears are frozen in place. Feet
Slip   the body falls…
Shins are skinned on the jagged stone.
Hands, panic-cold   reach   grasp
For the guideline, a frayed hope in the blasting
Wind, too eager to toss us to the brine.
Foot   follows   foot
                    and the land is left behind.

    The land, O the land…
        sunsets and springtimes
            long hair and slender wrists
                lemonade, peaches and sherbet
                    in the April orchard.
    Memories, as soft as the stroke
        of a robin's breast, memories…
            the lilac, dahlia, the magnolia
                the rose, the pear tree sighing
                    her petals in the moonlit dawn.

                    GONE

The mind strains the body seaward toward
The iron cross at the jetty's end where
        the shark is lurking…
        where the manta slithers…
        where the whale waits with open jaws.
Again the foot slips   and yet again.
Until sobbing and bleeding on the last gray rock
The worn body crawls upon its cross…
                    commending its spirit to the sea.

The living cannot enter here, cannot
Pierce the veil of light, protecting their sight
From the entrance to the tomb and the womb.
The dead enter here, following the dead
In slow procession through the sea…
The dead follow the dead who are followed
By the dying and the not-yet born.
Faces frontal, they proceed like pharaohs
Groping in the shadows for abandoned thrones.
Those who remain behind do not remain behind
Though like sobbing ghosts they drift
Over the land…believing only in the land…
Grasping and embracing the land, denying the sea…
They follow, with their eyes longing landward
Tripping and stumbling over the jetty stones.
They stumble…they falter…they are gone.
They linger…they dream…they are born.
Those who enter here are desperate…
Stripped of their palaces, of their thrones.
Stripped of their countries, of their homes.
Stripped of their families, of their wives.
Stripped of their bodies, of their lives.
Those who enter here are stripped of gods.
Those who enter here leave their blood
To mingle with the sea, their bodies at
The jetty's end…they possess nothing…
Those who enter here seek for no thing…
Those who enter here are no thing…
Those who enter here, enter here alone.

Beneath the surface of the sea—ceasing and becoming—
Cease to be. Here is the non-time between moments
Of time that stretches from death to birth. Entering
Here we perfect in wisdom all that we only knew in
The pilgrimage of the flesh. We die to be alive
On the silent side of time.
And dying we are born
Dead among the dead, veils of light, moving through
The shadows of the night…burning…purging our shadows
In the shadows, seeking union with the Virgin Light
That shone upon the waters and willed the stars aflame.
And the unifying light
Encircled by the night, contained in the forms
Of the twilight day of flesh is not consumed by night
But eludes our outward sight throbbing in the hollows
Of our hearts. We are drawn through the night
By the Cause and Source of light, to be swallowed
Into light and awaken at a new annunciation.

The Joy of Life

The garden is a choir of silence:
Dew drops trembling on the buds,
Crows perched in the trees, vapor
Ascending, shadows taking flight.
An eagle circles in the heavens.
Everything waiting.   Everything breathing.
Light swallows dark.   The land gives birth.

O April, April daybreak in the garden
The soil whispers promises of moisture and life.
The snows have surrendered; streams wash
The mountains. Over is the winter;
Gone the time of strife. Roses will be blooming
By the watercourse and soon, the butterfly
Will spread its wings, abandon its cocoon.

I waken from my time of dying.
I leave my beatific sleep.
I rode the sun the wide night flying
Beneath the earth, the hollow deep.
I rode until I found my Father
And my Mother in the night, bridged
The gulf of their desire, assuming
Flesh at the dawning of the light.

Mother is lovelier than all the dawns.
She is the chalice of all the myths and Mays.
She strolls among the flowers on this prettiest
Of days. She sits and sings, her young head tilted
And weaves a veil of blue and white. She knows
That I am coming, her songs are sighs
of her soul's delight.

Here is the cradle of eternity, the source
Of the seasons and the stars. The fig
And date are ripe at the roadside, it is
Springtime on the road to Ain-Karim.

I am the bride of the wind! O my cousin.
The tulips at your window have sprung from
Humble bulbs; so am I: the dark soil from which
The whitest rose shall come. I am the night

That contains the morning star, the pool filled
With water of sunlight. I am the nest at
The summit of Horeb. The eagle has landed
Leaving me with wings that urge me heavenward.

Throw wide your doors, O my cousin, my friend.
The sun has filled your house and mine, has pierced
Your shadow and mine, light has shone in our
Darkness…love has taken flesh in our wombs.

We are the lamps, my cousin, bearing forth
The light. Embrace me! Dance! Laugh! Weep for joy!
The eagle has entered our darkest night
That we might give flesh to his wondrous light.

Spirit dreamed and the universe became.
Mind and matter are one epiphany.
Before time was, the wind moaned over
The land, over the water, roaming aimlessly
Without beginning in the endless night.
Light became and light birthed life.
Life in matter is one epiphany. Spirit
Dreams and the universe becomes.

                                    O holy
Night, night shimmering with divinity,
Aves of the moon cooling the anxious earth,
Stars, harmonies of flickering ecstacies,
Spasms in the womb of the night…

        Hail woman, your friend is with you!
        But how, how might he comfort you?
        Your soul resplendent in virginity
        Your body full in birth's extremity
        At the summit of your femininity?
        Hail woman your friend is with you!

The mind dreaming everywhere is dreaming here.
Here is the epiphany in sweat screams and hair.
The flower of the pubis is opening, aching,
Bleeding in the agony of birth…

Spirit dreams and a human child is born.
Soul and body are one epiphany. Before time,
Before light, before life from light became,
This thought was, this flesh was, and this
Thought, this flesh became life of you and me.
We two, in love, are one epiphany. O my child,
Mind and matter, soul and body, woman and man,
These are one epiphany.
                            Forever fresh, forever
Spring, the female and the rosebud opening.
Eternal life is blossoming. Spirit/God is dreaming.
Eternal life is blossoming in this most holy night.

O Nameless Being
Being-In-Motion
Being-In-Things

Song sung in all, song
Of the beginning,
Springing universe
Caroling of stars
Burning psalm, turning
Galaxies, nebulae…
Beginning song: AAUUMM

Come unspoken speech
We beseech Thee, breach
The ocean womb of night.
O light   come   reach
To the broken womb
Of flesh, dispel
The night   O wholey Light.

Child, sung rhyme of love
Chime of joined desires
Born of the unborn gyre
Flung fire, spoken song
Choired of the night
Acquiring the dawn, the
Dew drops and the light…

The willing light
Spark spilling Mother
Father, the one Light
Willing you, my hymn
My trilling thrill
To die, die to night
And rise, rise to light.

O Nameless Being
Being-In-Motion
Being-In-Things

Come.

The Way of Sorrow and Death

This vision drifted to the bones of me:
The new Earth, born of the universe,
Fresh as a seed in an April furrow.
Birth–wet, womb–washed trembling with urgency,
A bursting breast of Spirit, bubbling
And breeding life in one raucous thrill
Of croaking, barking, belching, of trilling
In the whip–poor–will, unashamed jenny–donkey
Of an Earth braying among the stars.
This vision drifted through the bones of me:
A time before time before night before day,
Before man before murder and lying held sway,
Before rich before poor before poor became prey,
Before war killed the weak before blood–poisoned May,
Before war caused the soul of the Earth to decay,
O my child, my child within this temple this day
A vision drifted to the soul of me.

Devils lurk beneath the skin of our lives,
Growling behind our smiles, howling in our dreams…
Herpes on the body of the Earth, erupting…
Leaking the fluids of all death, erupting…
Rotting the bandages of government and trade.
War is drinking the blood of the poor!
Poisons are eating the flesh of the helpless!
Angry men of Babylon, greedy men of Rome!
Do you deny the Spirit? Do you yet deny?

This vision soaked into the soul of me…
O Nineveh..Nineveh the beautiful…
O Nineveh the just, city on a hill
Nation under God…Is your house to remain
In desolation? Are your blessings only
For your gluttony, your plenty for anxiety,
For fear, your sciences for violence and death?

Lawyers, judges smug behind black robes, called
To capture justice in the language of the law;
Where are the children? Where are the preborn young?

Are all hearts plundered of their innocence?
Is the body strengthened by piercing it again?
What have we done to the innocents?
Decay Invades The Heart! Decay Invades The Soul!
What have we done to the preborn young?
Doctors…Are my people cattle counted for cash?
Are you monsters? Money–grubbing maggots
On the bodies of the poor? Who among you serves?
Who sins against the Spirit? That Spirit questions you!

Leaders of the nations east, west, north and south,
Premiers, Prime Ministers and Presidents.
Do you curse the dawn light with your threats?
The twilight with your bombs and weaponry?
Strutting boasters, bloated bags of putrefaction.
Do you hold the helpless ones in fear?
The weak ones wasting in despair?
The Earth in bondage to your arrogance?
The time has come for your reply, you great ones!
The time has come for you to tear your hair!

A vision drifted to the bones of me,
Of all men naked in a failing sun.
Our fathers left us no inheritance.
No truths are seen to be self–evident.
Forgive me, my children, forgive me!
The flowers are fading; the wind becoming still.
We have yet these moments that we share
Before we find how different we are,
When I shall be an alien in your dreams…
Foreign and afraid…a failure and absurd.
Forgive us all, a people whose blasphemy
Is just about to snicker from their lips.

This vision drifted through the soul of me:
I saw the Earth as fresh as babies' breath,
And then in this very temple this very day I saw
The Earth approach the moment of her death.

At midnight, between winter and spring, after
The last leaf has fallen and is still, before
The early blossom has pierced the cerement,
Death beckons from the yonder shore as stars
Flicker in the dark like fireflies in some
Abandoned tomb. I awakened trembling
In the womb of night, not from but to
An unfamiliar dream. I wandered from my
Mother's house, a fugitive, a man alone.
The seasons had come and gone…

                                Aprils

Made their promises, the seed aching with
Urgency, roots throbbing with lust, blood
Pounding in the heart, then rains forgiving
The land. Summers shimmered beneath the tree,
The cicada wailing and funnels of insects
Dancing in the cooling radiance of dusk.
Autumns, the air whining in the dying light,
Harvests and the clear cooling of the night
Smelling of apples, melons and of hay…
The seasons came and slipped away…

                             February

Found me frightened beneath the stars, alone
Among the shadows of a world no longer real.
I am called to cleanse the windows to the sun!
A man forlorn, I hear a solitary song
Sung before the dawning of the sun…
Sung below the singing of the sea…
The melody of morningsong, the song
The morning glory sings, song of the breeze..
The morningsong…Spiritsong…the evensong…
The seasons have come and gone…

                             come and gone.

Under the lash…
The insects of panic scurry
And dart in the singing heat
Dig and sting beneath my skin.
The sap of terror drools like
Grease, sweating from the core
Of my brain, running down my skull
Under the lash.

Under the lash…
Bombs of agony flares of shame
Explode, illuminating
The midnight mausoleum of my heart,
Thrusting in light the sprawling
Landscape, the acres of my guilt…
Laughing tombs lurching forth their bile
Under the lash.

Under the lash…
Foul glories of all rottenness
Darkness covering the sun…
Sin sweats stinking from every pore,
An arch of devils covers me,
Wounding the core of me…
Trampling the greening spring of me
Under the lash.

Under the lash…
Sunken eyes darken in their caves
The tongue decays in the mouth hole.
The skin is parting; insects scurry out.
Ulcers fester on my heart's skin.
My seed goes putrid within my sex.
Abomination rots within my gut…
Under the lash.

Under the lash…
My heart slams against my chest pleading
"Let me out. O please, let me out."
The Earth spreads her legs awaiting
The phallus of the new born sun.
My fists pounding on the graveyard gate
"Let me in. O please, let me in."
Under the lash.

◆ 13 ◆

My dreams, my schemes and all my years are
Strewn on the landscape of my innocence
Crippling the splendor of the spring.

I am powerless. My hands are bound. Flames leap
From my heart, memories howl and puncture me
And pierce my brain like a crown of thorns…

Bleeding me, bleeding the blood of me.
Why do you shriek? Why do you bruise me?

I saw light! Light transfiguring the air…
Angels were dancing in the valley! What vast
Delusion was this? What rantings of a mind

Gone mad? What failure? Was it all some
Groaning dream, the cry of unconscious powers
For deliverance? Was it all delirium?

Was it all just fancies hung in the air?
Hallucinations? All just utter madness?
I await my death ashamed of my life.

I am cold and hot, thirsty and beyond
The want of drink. A sparrow tossed to dogs.

Father, where are you? Mother, where are you?

Where are you?   Where are you?

I am ashamed.

Called to cleanse the windows to the sun…
Staggering beneath
This yoke, my soul sorrowing, whimpering
aloud, melting in
The flames of terror, whining, my knees tremble
weaken and give in.

This dawn, precious, fresh, grieving with death…
The door is hurled ajar.
Squinting, my eyes receive their faces, born
cursing and raving
From the dark, familiar faces whose names
elude my memory.

Like a drunkard…foot follows foot…Pins
of pain pierce the marrow
Of my feet. I move in shadows. Weakness
chisels at my core
I sicken…I fall. Face down I smell,
and taste the kind Earth.

Rising I proceed toward light. Laughter, taunting.
They say "we love you"
Then they spit on me. I forgive them…
accept their ridicule.
I accept the spit of "I love you,"
the darkness and the pain.

A spasm shivers through my nerves. Beneath
the shadow of this
Tree, I fall. My nose bleeds in the dust. My
back splits, the bone shows.
Riots of pain howl though my brain. Despair
invades. I vomit.

Goaded by growling ghouls, the torment resumes.
My limbs rebel at
My command to enter into light.
Every movement is
Exquisite with pain. The voices blend
to one ferocious groan.

Within the shade of this great tree, I fall,
my lips gasping blood.
Even the pain is muffled now. I cannot
stand. Then a damp cloth
Is pressed against my brow, a cup to my mouth.
My sister…My sister…

The light is brighter than the pain. All is
unimportant now.
I embrace the loneliness, the exile
the taunting, the trail
Of liars on either side before me…
and…I accept you.

◆ 15 ◆

I grieve.   I mourn.   I lament.   I moan.
All hands are covered with blood and the odor
Of evil wanders through the land. The whole
Head is sick, the heart gone faint gone flabby.
All kneel frigid before the works of our hands.
All become still more greedy for profit.
The soil stinks of death. The soil cannot sustain
A culture gone mad.

                    Our leaders mislead us, my people.
They destroy the road that we walk upon.
With wiles, wealth and weaponry they secure
Their hold on this heap of ruins, this planet
Of our shattered dreams. They speak and they speak
And they speak and their speech is utter madness.

Our children choke on the dust of a dying Earth.
I grieve.   I mourn.   I lament.   I moan.
They are starving in the shadows of our weaponry.
The children cry for bread and we give them bombs!
The Horror!   The Horror!   The Horror!
The heavens and the Earth are in mourning.
The heavens and the Earth are pining away.

From a distant radio…
"What have we done to the Earth?
What have we done to our fair sister?
Ravaged and plundered and ripped her and bit her,
Stuck her with knives in the side of the dawn and
Tied her with fences and dragged her down.
I hear a very gentle sound…with your ear down
To the ground…We want the world and we want it
Now?.........................NOW!!!!!!!!!!!!!"

We sleep and beneath us is a bed of maggots,
Over us a blanket of worms. Woe to you
Ravager never ravaged, plunderer never plundered,
To those who call evil good and good evil,
Call darkness light. You see nothing, understand
Nothing and so will be put to shame. Weep, weep
For the country filled with darkness and distress.
Mourn for the country whose light flickers out.

The visions of our poets are delusions,
Tinsel things, scrap heaps of word tricks
And much academic Blah Blah Blah, never
Pointing to the Lie: our love of death.
Their images are lies and cannot stem
Our agony. Vanity we pursued and so vanity
We became. The disaster spreads from
Nation to nation…..THE HORROR!

My country…My planet…anguish gnawing
At my heart, each beat leaving its bruise.
And at whom are you jeering? Are you not
The spawn of lies? Is not the pretence
Of your integrity like filthy clothing?
Descending to the heart of night, I plunge
To the core of hell, joining all who dwell
In shadows…

Me and my shadow
Strollin' down the avenue…

The moist mouth of the tomb spits out its dead:
The first is a strutting braggart twirling
His baton…

Me and my shadow
Strollin' down the avenue…

The second, his dead skin dripping with sweat,
His quivering lips twisted to a grin, hands
In the heat of greed, he rubs his coins.
He's counting and counting and longing for more.

O me and my shadow
Strollin' down the avenue…

The tomb clears its throat, rattles up its phlegm.
The third struggles from this foul slime. He recites
What he writes on rest room walls. His right hand
Is thrust within his pants.

Me and my shadow
Strollin' down the avenue…

Threats, curses, and laughter are heard from the dead
Belly of hell. The lion bares his teeth but his heart
Is made of cheese. He watches the raping of the woman.
He drools and trembles in his glee.

Tra la la la
Me and my shadow
Strollin' down the avenue…

The fifth is a giggling mass of cellulite, an eclair
In either hand. Behind him a noodle of dung stretches
Back to the lips of hell.

O me and my shadow
Strollin' down the avenue…

A sixth staggers into the light, his eyes flashing
Like a rat's. He preaches on "The spiritual advantage
Of poverty." When he's done, he turns, howling
And shaking with his laughter.

Me and my shadow
Strollin' down the avenue...

Moaning, crying and pleading are heard. A wagon
Is drawn by war–crippled and greed–starved children.
Upon this wagon the seventh rides sleeping. His
Abdomen is spread upon a bed. His hands are shiny
With the dead jellies of his lust. The air around
Him is a halo of his stench.

O me and my shadow
Strollin' down the avenue.

◆ 17 ◆

Into the tomb, the pregnant womb of darkness.
Descend the stairway that leads beneath the floor.
All is blue and white, the Earth seen from space.
Stair by stair, terror eclipsing my heart
The silence growing louder as I go down. Thicker,
The air is sickening. Fear broadcasting, rising
To a whine. Acid vomit creeping up my throat.
There is a casket in the center of the vault.
The room is muffled and hot with faded velvet.
But the room is everywhere busy with whispering.
Thought is spiralling toward delirium: My Casket!
A nest of bats explodes! Fiends dance on air!
I open the lid; stare with fascinated glee.
My heart is throbbing in my temples and eyeballs.
My child! My battered child! My dead buried child!
I drag him out. I hold him to me. I press him in.
He awakens. His arms are gathered tight around me.
We kiss and kissing he has melted into me.
Then a blast of light! The floor falls away!
When I awaken I am drifting among the stars!

Meeting the Father

"You have plunged to the bowels of the night,
To the land at the bottom of the sea.
You have come to the unifying light,
Where—ceasing and becoming—cease to be.
You are born on the other side of time,
Where nothingness explodes and brings to birth,
At the sound of the universal chime,
The galaxies, the supernovae, Earth.
You have journeyed where heroes come alone,
Have surrendered your spirit to the Wind,
Have stepped beyond the final jetty stone,
To blessing more original than sin.
      So here is the Heart of cosmogenesis…
      All that is is 'IS' 'HERS' is 'IS' 'HIS' is 'IS'."

Resurrection and the Goddess

◆ 19 ◆

O stars stars stars effusion of sparks bellowed from the dark
brilliance of the cock-crowing Godhead,
Spawn born of yawning dawn, first outburst bursting from
the bulbous belly of the fireball, glowing
Profusion of syllables, silver and yellow exploding in
the vast night of nothingness.
All in all, first trumpet call, windfall of atoms, of light
cascading delight in

the luminous, numinous night. Galaxies, galaxies of galaxies
turning, quasars and pulsars
Pulse burning and dying. Rising vortices of ecstacies
and angels butterflying
On hydrogen winds, wild, whipped and whistling, green dragons
wandering fogs, roses dreaming
Through the undying, unifying womb of God; praying labia part
whispering the first murmur,

The starting sigh beginning the innocent universe. Cities
of light sparkle at the edge
Of the heavens. Comets career in flight pioneering into
the fertile twilight. O holy
Holy dark, ark of all covenants, bark of beauty too piercing
for scrutiny, trinity
And virginity pregnant and glistening with divinity.
Hail chalice! Hail holy Light!

Yearning arms thrown wide gather exploding roses sown and blown
in the wild womb of wonder.
The hands of the cornerstone finger the rosaries of the stars.
The pregnant heart of God groans
Overblown, birthing the Heart of Light, ground of the soul
and soil of the ground of the Earth…
As yet a foal, the foal of a donkey with its Fool, incapable
of self-control. Transfigured

Face of space, happy in His rigmarole. Face of my face, face
without hint of disgrace…
Ocean eyes beholding with delight the original grace, the
unborn face still smiling, still
Reconciling when I no longer shape my face but silent, slip
undefiling into the one
Blissful sea of being, gleaming with the one Light that in
the beginning was the Word.

◆ 20 ◆

Let me part the veil enshrouding your comeliness…
Let me breathe upon you, to soothe the stings of their
Iniquity. Come rise with me O loveliest of all
The planets, how welcoming, how delightful is your bed!

Poppies bob in your meadows; peach trees blush in your
Valleys. Buds blossom and your fruit is sweetness to my
Tongue. I come, my bride, my beautiful, my lovely one.
The winter is past, the time of melodies has begun.
Salmon leap and the dove is heard once more…the human
Has outgrown the need for war; the veil of shadow is parted,
My princess among the stars. Show me your face my fair…
I hear your voice. It is soft and your song wonderful.

Before the dawn…before shadows flee…I return to
The planet of all my covenants. You ravish my heart
My sister, my promised bride. You smell of cinnamon
And every fragrance…how beautiful you are…

How delicious is your flesh, how fragrant your perfume.
Honey and milk are your garments, my garden planet,
My fountain of delights. Orchards of pears, pomegranates
Peaches and plums are yours and every wondrous aroma!
Rise ye dawn winds! Breathe your breath over my beautiful;
Announce all of her perfumes! I come again to my
Garden, to my bride. Open to me my sister, my tears
Are morning's dew, I am resplendent as the sun. Open to me.

Before the dawn...before shadows flee...I return to
The planet of all my covenants. You ravish my heart
My sister, my promised bride. You smell of cinnamon
And every fragrance...how beautiful you are!

I gaze at you O daughter of the King, willows
Bowing to the wind, deep oceans teeming with life..
Birds calling from the darkness of the forest:
"Come to me." You are my nest among the galaxies.
Your breathing is sweeter than apples. I return to
Your fields, cities and villages. See, the vines are
In bloom, the grapes grow plump. In the morning I bring
To you the riches I have stored for my beloved one.

Let me part the veil enshrouding your comeliness...
Let me breathe on you to soothe the stings of their
Iniquity. Come rise with me O loveliest of all
The planets; how lovely, how delightful is your bed!

◆ 21 ◆

My Husband, be an ointment soothing me. Our
Children have abused and plundered me; restore
me for I exult in you. Protect me in your
embrace and let your cloak drawn around me be
love. My Wife, fairest daughter of the King,
implore the children with these words of mine.
Tell them in the name of spirit and matter, of
the dawnlight and twilight, in the name of the
heavens and the earth...

To come to me, for I engendered the universe and am
Emerging in the blood of the stars. Our children are the
Earth conscious of her splendor. They must abandon
Themselves to her self, their songs to her harmonies.
They must ask themselves if their attitudes and actions
Injure the epiphanies of the planet, impeding the
Emergence of life. They must acknowledge to each other
And to me the greedy venom of their delusions and long
To have their delusions delivered. I yearn to cool the
Fever of their hysteria. They must acknowledge the ways

They have harmed the creation and strain in their
Efforts at healing all life. Then, I will refresh the
Garden I designed for their delight. They must continue
Their self-scrutiny, acknowledge their myopia and
Nurture the emergence of love. If they cherish my bride,
The planet and encourage this respect in others, I will
Renew their Joy and renew the face of the Earth. Tell
Them to come to me...come...

My husband comes to me in the first light of a
Fresh creation, emerging in the depths of my
Seas, rising and rending the shadow of my evil
Night. He heals and cheers me with the
Laughter of his heart. Awake ye winds! Awake
Ye waters! Awake Ye meadows! My husband
Returns to the garden Of his delights. I
Tremble at the entry of my Lord. He eats of my
Fruits. I am my beloved and my beloved is I.

◆ 22 ◆

Spirit emerges from the moist pod of the Earth womb
Past the bleeding gate to the screaming glare
Of solar day. Birth is the primary rite, first
Of all sacraments.
          True, men have their marvels:
The vulva of joined hands, thumb to thumb,
Index to index, birth canal for the Triune
Majesty made food for a famished world.
          But, soft
In the folds of the planetary uterus burns
The old heat, the pounding blood of the galaxies.
Blinded by the sun we forgot the Earth. Earth heat
And solar heat are one fire. Earth flesh and solar
Flesh are one. Earth is spouse to the sun.
          All women
Bleed the ancient blood. All women birth the ancient
Flesh. Women give eyes to the galaxy. All women
Mother the spirit, are midwives to the universe.

Hail Holy Queen, Mother of the galaxies,
Of the stars, of the Earth and anthem of the light
Mother of Spirit sighing with many melodies
      Through the kind breast of the continents
Mother of every mercy, eucharist of flesh
Mother of breasts heavy with the milk of compassion
Mother of anguishes and caresses, of breathing
      Pines that kiss the mouths of the dead.
Mother of matter and mother of time, of beating
Hearts and wings, most gracious advocate, mother
Of the Spirit, mother of wind in the grains
      Mother of love, of decency and hope
Mother of flowers and grasses in the meadows,
Of graveyards busy with whispering. Mother of silence
Of forests with the cry of birds, of the tomb and womb
      Mother of gathering and drifting clouds
Mother of the jetty and the journey through the sea
Mother of soils and mother of souls, we have sickened
And we are sorrowful and again we come to thee.

The New Story

Myriad and everlasting were the eternities
of the Great Heart's broodings; fecund was the silence
of His yearning. Time gushed from timelessness when
the Lone Heart burst, a triumph of surrender, a
wincing spasm of pain-pierced ecstasy, light rending
the curtain of non-being in a scorching choir
of the One and undivided word:

BECOME   BECOME   BECOME

My odyssey is the odyssey of the universe.
The forms that spring from the ancient fire are forms
of the becoming me! O fountainhead of energy
genesis, squirting the juice of light from the Great Heart
in blazing geysers that cool to sentient dust,
still soaked with mind, ecstasy, caprice and all
the roaring passions of the Birthing Heart, spiralling
profusions of incarnate Love swamping the emptiness.
O Supreme Orgasm of delight splashing into
the womb, we shake, we quiver as we rejoice in You!

My journey is the journey of the Milky Way!
The dance in Andromeda is the dance of me!
O galaxies of galaxies, O whirling winds
of radiance and elation, O grand pinwheels
of love, playthings of the Innocent Heart, coiling
and amassing the yearning dust. O empires of
the stars, fulfilling the darkness. O arms of light
ardent for embrace, pregnant and approaching
the fullness of their nova term, shaking like an
April seed and screaming the creative Word…

LIGHT   LIGHT   LIGHT

The Word of agony that would birth the worlds, contracting,
contracting, bright and brighter still, until, in one
paroxysm of splendor, one convulsion of delight
they burst, strewing mind-powder sparkling throughout the vast
expanse. Again the yearning and new empires of light,
dying stars rising from the dead…and here was born
"The Light of the Planets" "The Husband of the Earth"…

HAIL   FATHER   SUN!

◆ 25 ◆

Father sun in the boyhood of his brilliance began
to glow. The young star boasted promises in hot-hearted
aves that crooned the cosmic dawn. Deep within
the sun, Great Heart yearned lusts that thrilled to wakefulness
the gathering dust. Within all the swirling
sentience, the ancient dawn began to glow.
The gathering of the Earth is the gathering of me.
O April April, it is springtime in the cosmos,
the Virgin Earth awakens to the kisses
of the sun. The maiden Earth is pirouetting,
in her ecstasy begetting the promises
of every life in unison. Fires raged
within the heart of her. Blushing and surrounded
by the omming halo of her radiance, she received
within the folds of her flesh, the hot phallus of the sun.

In her zest the teenage Goddess roared.
In outbursts of bombast she spewed moist heat
through all the pain-red pores of her puelline skin.
She whirled, her body assuming her shape, while
the lava of her early bleeding flowed hot. The grand
dandy sun yearned to the young Goddess with all
the longing of the Great Heart within him. This same
longing shimmered from her deepest core, cooling
to a veil surrounding her. She whirled and glowed, her
kind face tilted and formed a veil of blue and white.

She knew within that life was coming, her sighs
were songs of her soul's delight. From mists came rains,
soothing baths for a sultry queen. Insights of
lightning flashed, flamed and flared. As her passion
calmed, her halo cooled to a still and moving glow.

Allured by the longing moon, the oceans heaved and lurched,
pitched and lunged, sleepless, a lover alone at midnight.
Tide-trembled thrills shuddered over the bright skin
of the swashing Goddess. In shooting fonts, fiery lands
formed and dissolved. To and fro, surge and ebb
the heaving ocean rolled, striking beat upon beat
and hurling wind-driven waves that crested, smashed
and splashed back the salty wash. Then hot shores
and angry mountains began to cool, some enduring
the day-long lapping of the swells. Pangaea arose
from the moving waters. Against these rocks in later
ages would press the grip of hoof, foot, and claw. Down
these jetties sojourners would journey to the sea.
For centuries of ages the sun nurtured the shaking
sea womb. Shapes emerged, tried, and disappeared.

New shapes formed in the sloshing broth, seething with
promises. Dreams dancing in and out of dust, groped
grouped and passed away. Steam rising in angry
shouts, cooled and fell in whisperings. Clouds gathered
and dispersed, gathered and dispersed. In all of this
the faint light of yearning glimmered, a memory
of dark origins in the Great Heart. Forms and forms
flowed over the waves, dreams drifted through the heat.
Dust gathered unto dust. The greater the forms,
the greater the calling to form. The brighter shone
the glow, the clearer the memory of that calling.
Suddenly, and everywhere were shapes that lived!
The Great Heart yearned and the universe became.
Mind and matter are one epiphany.
The Great Heart yearns and the universe becomes.

I unfold all my buds to you, beloved; they
blossom, eager to eat the laughing light of your
love. I open my leaves to you, O Thou whose
radiance scatters the shadows of night, kissing all
the meadows of my belly into song. I spread
all my branches too; I feel your heat in every nest,
in every lodge, nook, lair, den and aerie of me,
my heart trembling beneath its scales, its fur and its down.
Under the soils, my roots shudder in dark waters.

I sing to you, pointed in every throat, piercing
the mists of forests, O Thou, burning well of my
memory. Mine, the OM of harmonies hummed by
insects flashing and darting in the April morning.
Mine, the dance of the dragonflies, the slow warning
of the wasps. I low, mouth and teeth frothing green,
teats swollen with sweetness. Mine the skittish spark in
the eye, the flight of the hooves. I slither across
the noon rocks, expose my belly, and wait for you.

I shriek to you in the night, the sudden teeth, talons,
the disbelief. I go numb and give my flesh to you;
I surrender; I too am food. Hungry elsewhere,
I howl over the the lonely miles of the night; I scurry
through moonlight and shadow. In a spasm of screams,
feathers, and leaves, I find you and tear you for
my young. Shivering before dawn, I huddle: monkey,
gorilla, chimpanzee, and the apes with bloody teeth
who fill the graves of their dead with my blossoms.

In the midst of murmuring moonlight, my tribe
undulates to the pounding dictates of the drums.
My shaman in mystic psychosis, circles
the blazing axis of village life. Writhing,
the ring of dancing, sweat-shining bodies, flickers with
leaping tongues of light. From my shaman, circles of power
tremble outward through the dancers, their huts and beyond...
through the forest peering through a thousand eyes...
outward, engulfing the planet...engulfing the sun...
engulfing the turning galaxy...engulfing the universe.

My shaman is the place of entry; my shaman's
life is sacred time. Beneath the wolf's head mask, forms
pour through the torn curtain of his mind, flooding
outward in wakan rings, food for the human family.
Here is the dreaming of Great Heart, yearning
from the ancient fire. Grace rumors over the tribe.
The One Song sings in all, song of the beginning,
springing universe, caroling of the stars,
the burning psalm, turning galaxies and nebulae...
the beginning song: AAAAAAUUUUUUMMMMMM

A shriek! All eyes are fixed on the holy one. The tribe
awaits my speech of reassurances. His eyes
are fierce with authority. See, he leaps and struts,
circling the fire, glaring at one, glaring at another,
melting all in the flames of his gaze. A shriek!
Silence! I speak: "I am Mother, the midnight moon,
the wind in the grains, the music in the pines. I am
the ocean flickering in the dawn, the scream in the forest,
the fire in your midst. I am the corn. I am the cave,
I am your milk and the welcome of your grave. I am Mother."

Great Mother Planet brought forth a daughter-people
priestess-children for Herself, natural, wholey,
whose dance was sunlaughter and moonsong and starrain,
a people whose feet prayed the dust prayer, whose skins bathed
in wetgrace, breathers of spiritfires, their bodies are
her soils, their breath, her winds; Her womb pulse is their blood.

Earth named Great Heart: WAKAN-TANKA

And Great Mother Planet birthed a sage so keen
that fables hold, he was born an elder, who
at the frontier of his exile wrote his book: "The mind
of Great Heart is like a bellows, breathing galaxies
of mind-dust into being, with the sun and his planet
who groans in birthing the wisdom of the myriad things."

Earth named Great Heart: TAO

There was born of Great Mother Planet a people
so astounded at the Presence as to name thousands
of gods and goddesses, which in unison could
proclaim not the least hint of that Luminosity,
a people so pregnant with memory and hope
that a million lifetimes seemed less significant than dew.

Earth named Great Heart: BRAHMAN

Great Mother Planet delivered a man so
confident that the human heart throbbed at the core
of creation, and rippled through the home, the city,
the nation, the earth, and the galaxy, as to dream
of cultures to tabernacle the Luminous,
making humans partners with earth and with the universe.

Earth named Great Heart: SINCERITY

And there was born of Great Mother Planet a prince
of such compassion for the whole agonizing tribe,
that he would nullify all the gods and goddess known,
that the One Love unknown could be felt shivering through
atoms, molecules, cells, hearts, nations, planets and stars,
in the one tremendous Song that could still the suffering.

Earth named Great Heart: MIND

Great Mother Planet brought forth a people
of the Original Journey, burning with fires
of prophecy, pregnant with the seed of Great Heart,
a people born to be the son, who parted the sea,
ate bread of the skies, a nation of patriarchs, prophets
and priests, who would dare to call Great Heart,"Father."

Earth named Great Heart: YAHWEH

And there was born of the Oneness of Great Heart
with the Blessed Virgin Earth, a son who sucked the body
and blood of the planet from the breasts of a woman,
a Son, Father of his Mother, born bloody and writhing,
and who died bloody and writhing to accomplish what
even He despaired of doing until he died and did.

Earth named Great Heart: JESUS

Great Mother Planet gave birth to a man aglow
with the miseries of so many missing fathers, that he
would plead for years in the cave of desperation,
beseeching Great Heart for fathering, and when the fire
of the Origin, suffused the cave of the Earth-womb,
he announced One Love in a scream whose ripples tremble still.

Earth named Great Heart: ALLAH

This is Newhaven. This is England. This is the Jetty.
Ascending through the surface of the sea, my vision
is encountered by these three: the fishing father
with his adolescent son, and the seagull
with folded wings who is kindred to the sun.

This is August. The fishermen who have come and gone
since morning, have stained the jetty with heads, tails
and guts, in sun-scabbed blood. Far away, radios pulse a
muted blare from the sands. Rainbows float upon the water.
The rattle and clank of the harbor deafen the day.

Here is Tidemills, town of broken forms and cracked
foundations. Wild broccoli claims forsaken streets
where the children ran. A carpet of condoms, bottles
and trash perdures, shed by the young who visit here,
to couple in union with the sea. This is Tidemills,

a rubble of pieces, dead hopes and shattered dreams,
a colloid of broken machines with rocks and weeds, coughed
up from the sea. The shrieking bird with flickering wings
still faces seaward, warning of the wind, warning
of the water, warning of the soils, while Tidemills

slips slowly into the sea. Beyond High Beach, Seaford…
the place of crossing from the sea. In Seaford I listened
to the horns mourning through the fog. I stared seaward
through the mist, longing for all the lost ancestors. From
Seaford, I saw our people, not evil, but lost, sleeping

to the droning of machines. Out at sea, the sludge
sloshes from the bowels of the ships. Seaford becomes
a sponge for all the blackness, oozing beneath the stones.
Seaford, this place of new beginnings, life crying
weak in whispers, amid all the clatter and the clank.

I went to Seaford Head, and there, staring seaward,
my face to the landward wind, high above all the clouds,
I saw the curve of the Earth and of the universe.
There I saw a dead life dissolved in the brine, sloughed
off in the journey through the sea. This is August...

the summer is in full flourish, the casino
is laughing from the gut: pinball, pinwheels, pop corn
and balloons. The people are smiling, contented and tanned,
dressed in yellows, orange, and red, walking their strutting
yappers, poodles, Pomeranians, and Pekingese, forms and
forms...

A Warning from the Earth

◆30◆

To The People Of Nineveh

I am Mother of all the mothers.
I am Mother of all the Marys.
I am Mother of all the fathers.
I am the Bride of Great Heart.

I am the Earth

…today I speak…
Disarm the entire planet….NOW.
Stop polluting the soils….NOW.
Stop poisoning the waters…NOW.
Stop degrading the air……NOW.
Stop ravaging the forests…NOW.
No longer desecrate the animals.
Stop killing the preborn young.

—or—

The heavens will withhold their showers and the soils will begrudge their bounty when they turn to dust. All life will undergo the great collapse of nature's increase. Famines will visit the life-planet like never before, starvation in all the lands where there was plenty. The waters will flush poisons over the land; all flesh will boil with hideous growths and stink in corruption. The stench will ascend to the highest atmosphere and will churn upon every wind. The bodies of monsters will appear among you and among the animals bodies not willed by Great Heart in the grand genesis of all beauty and all generosity since the beginning.

In The Beginning

We were dark, enfolded, in the infinite cold
of the Great Heart's lonely dreaming.
A dream within a dream within a dream unfurled,
the fireball and galaxies of stars
were hurled, in one spasm of delight Great Heart ended
endless night, the planet Earth
then life then human consciousness uncurled in an
everlasting scream that would
engender every dream: "HOC EST CORPUS MEUM."

There Was Light

The lightless, endless night became the rite of endless
morning, and cooled to dust adorning
our emerging galaxy. And I was with
the virgins in attendance
of the sun, who in his second birth would seed
my ceaseless pregnancies. I
harbored you within my heart, along with every
living thing. I formed a veil for all to
breathe, a veil to give you gathering. I made the rain
to fill the seas; I filled the soils
with ecstacies; I poured perfumes on every breeze
and filled the trees with harmonies.
The moon was midwife to the brine that rocked and sloshed
with energies. My one desire
was just to give, my only longing was to please.
The Great Heart with his spilling will
willed a thrill within my seas, that formed a billion willing
wives who birthed a billion trilling lives.

Then There Was Life

Dreaming dust married dreaming dust; plants and animals
appeared. My oceans burst aflame
with lives, my soils and then my atmosphere. I am
the snake who eats her tail; I am
the flabby mother whale. I am the breath that you
inhale; I am the mind of fairy-tale.
I am the tree who shelters you, the nourishment
you suck and chew. I am the teeming
ocean floor, the shark who lurks, The Ancestor.
I breathed within the dinosaur;
I was their life and death and more...I am the governed
and the governor. I am
the eagle and his flight, the insect and amphibian.
I am the moonlight and the night,
the monkey sleeping on the limb. I am the pelican
and gull and all that thrives on
every shore, the fish, the worm and the fisherman...
the Goddess who gave birth to man.

Then There Was Consciousness

And you, you are my darling ones, my laughing ones,
forever young. You are my dream
within my dream, your cultures are my mother-tongue.
And it is ours to praise the sun
through all the throats of every faith, ours to marvel
at the ONE of whom all creatures
are the wraith. In you I love all body-souls, all lands,
all rivers, sky and sea. But you
forget that I'm of Great Heart and you are born of me.

Will There Then Be Death?

Civilizations rise and fade away, rise and fade away, like leaves. With them the tyrants come and go and the greedy and the cruel. It begins with the destruction of the soil. People of Nineveh, I am not your whore! I have watched the soils die and turn to dust. I have watched the waters abort the lives for which they are the womb. I have seen the air at noon darken over the Great City. People of Nineveh I am not your whore! I have watched your machines devour the woodlands and wetlands the farmlands and meadowlands. The animals and children are dying. The birds and fish are dying. The planet of life becomes a tomb. People of Nineveh, I will watch you no more.

—for—

I am Mother of all the mothers.
I am Mother of all the Marys.
I am Mother of all the fathers.
I am the Bride of Great Heart.

I am the Earth.

…Great Heart speaks…

"Jonah is sent with this message:"

"Change or the Great City will collapse.
The human is to live, a single family
among the other families of Earth."
Let this be a warning unto you,
…a prophecy against you…

O people of Nineveh.